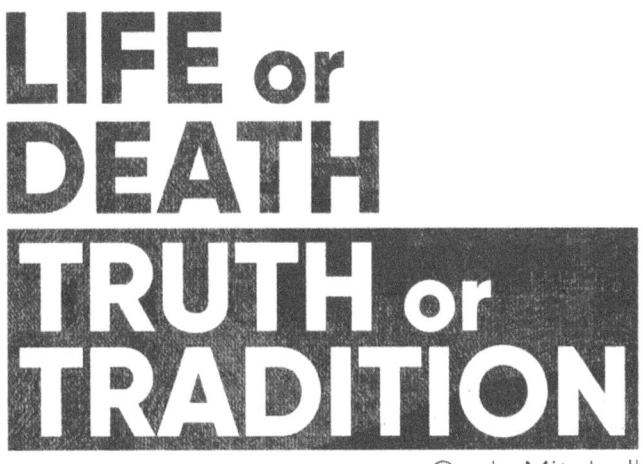

Cody Mitchell

LIFE or DEATH TRUTH or TRADITION

Copyright © 2021 Cody Mitchell
All rights reserved, including the right to reproduce this book or portions thereof in any form whatsoever.

For information email soulhousellc@gmail.com
www.soulhousellc.com

Cover Design by Mario Butterfield

ISBN:978-1-943014-02-6
Also available in ebook format

DEDICATION

Dedicated to TMH YHWH in heaven. To the parents, he created me from and anyone seeking citizenship in Heaven. Whether naturally by nationality and obedience, or being grafted in through obedience and acknowledgment. Finally, to Watchman Yahu and Deborah Yah who have been like second parents to me for years Halleluyah!!

"And may he renew his covenant with you. That you may be to Him a nation for His inheritance for all the ages, and that he may be to you and to your seed an Elohiym in truth and righteousness throughout all the days of the earth."
Jubilees 22:15

CONTENTS

	Introduction	1
1	Family	3
2	Sickness	6
3	The Most High	9
4	By His Name	15
5	The Covenant	24
6	The Commandments	30
7	Two Nations	44
	Afterword	50
	About the Author	57

INTRODUCTION

BEFORE YOU BEGIN reading this book, I must establish that it is for those seeking Heaven. If you are not, or if your focus is centered somewhere else, then—I love you nonetheless, but—this book is not for you. For those reaching toward Heaven as the ultimate priority, I first celebrate you for acknowledging that we have a Creator. I then want to remind you that we are to be seeking *Him*, and *His will* first in everything we do. I am aware of the battle between flesh and Spirit happening in your head and heart every day even as you sleep, for we are born of the flesh (Gal 5:19-21). To battle this, we must put on the Creator's whole armor and display the fruit of the Spirit found in Galatians 5: 22 & 23.

Today, many people's spirits have all but tapped out. Falling victim to unrighteous earthly desires and decide not to give true righteous dedication to their spirit, which is under attack by this Matrix-like system of lies and deception running the world we live in today. This body of ours is temporal, and whatever you experience will pass; your soul, however, is eternal, and that is where you should focus most of your thoughts and intentions. I will never be perfect—according to scripture, we all fall short—so in everything you read, seek truth and understanding for yourself. I pray my message here is received with love and peace. It is with urgency I deliver this message to you, sadly I'm aware that the majority will not hearken.

1 FAMILY

"...and ye shall return every man unto his family..." (Leviticus 25:10)

I CONSIDER MYSELF to be a rather meek individual, mostly due to a strong Christian upbringing. My dad always had a Bible in his hand as early as I can remember quoting scriptures and teaching lessons to everyone in his presence. He is the most committed Heaven seeker I still know of today; at 34 years old, I find his leadership to be priceless. Mom, on the other hand, took care of the household and anyone who found themselves in her presence. She is the strongest servile spirit I know of, in all my days I still have not known someone like her, and I strive to mimic her in how I care for others.

Both of my parents are blessings, but childhood was far from perfect. I grew up alongside an older brother, 3 sisters (one younger, 2 older), and an uncle just 4 years my senior in a small apartment. We created a life full of memories still held today. Disregarding money, I could not have asked for anything better growing up. When I turned 12, we got our first house, which was a delight, and shortly after that, my brother (a local university star) was drafted into the NBA, and life appeared to be lining up to our dreams as a family unit. I understand now Satan is always working, and nothing is *happily ever after* until Heaven appears once and for all. Follow along as I quickly reveal the next few years of my young adulthood that were filled with pain and struggle, soon followed by knowledge and freedom.

After a few years in the league, my brother went to jail and did 3 years as a first-time offender, and the family began to separate for various reasons, including my uncle who distanced himself after marriage. This was incredibly difficult for me because I had never been close to anyone like I was with my uncle, and sadly we still talk very little today.

Around 2010, things got confusing when my dad had a change of heart about his understanding of the Bible. He removed all ties to the church we were members of for the past 15-20 years. With this, he also removed all ties to holidays as well, and this was hard for mom, who was attached to Christmas in particular, but she followed dad's lead. I was not living at the house at the time but pops decided to separate himself when others had trouble with the new changes he had committed to. This came as a surprise to anyone connected to my family; because *we* were the grounding place for others to find peace and understanding. Many were convinced a spirit made its way into my dad, but I could not believe this about him; he had always been a living example of someone searching for truth and righteousness.

Over the next few years, mom lost the house, and everyone went their own way, which was also sad and unbelievable. We had built a reputation of being such a strong and blessed household, and there were many families with close relations leaning on us, but life continues on. I kept meeting with pops at his new address because he's my dad, and again I knew his soul was always searching for the truth. We would get together to read the Bible and discuss scriptures, many of which I found were not being upheld by the church or the masses. In this chapter of my life, I also began dealing with health issues, which kept me in prayer but distanced me from the Bible for lack of abilities.

2 SICKNESS

"For a just man falls seven times, and rises up again: but the wicked shall fall into mischief." (Proverbs 24:16)

I QUICKLY BECAME DEBILITATED days after a Tetanus shot. For a while, I went blind in one eye, but shortly after it appeared to heal, I woke up with the inability to walk or even talk for some time. Surviving only by faith I continued doing everything I could to pay my bills before being diagnosed with Multiple Sclerosis. According to the doctor, it was urgent that I put my faith in 1 of 3 or 4 medications quickly or a wheelchair appeared likely by the age of 30. I was 27 years old when diagnosed on May 28th, 2014, which just so happened to be world MS day. If interested I wrote a book on this chapter of my life called *"From Disease to Freedom"*. Long story short, in elaborate timing, I discovered that these medications would merely bandage my issues at best and lead to further susceptibility to even worse conditions in my future, only enslaving me to more pharmaceuticals and taking my hard-earned money in the process. I'm truly convinced I'd be fine had I not taken the advice to get a Tetanus shot.

Over the years with much analysis, research, and revelation; I've come to understand that nothing in this world asides from the words of The Most High (TMH) found in the bible today are Holy (morally and spiritually righteous), therefore all things that have been accepted by this world must be evaluated daily. We have been forewarned Satan is the prince of this world, and he is also the father of lies and deception, therefore we must take a moment to acknowledge this as fact and stay on guard.

James 4:4 says friendship to the world is enmity with (TMH). Whoever therefore seeks friendship with the world is an enemy of TMH. Timothy 3:16 & 17 says, all scripture is by inspiration of TMH, and is profitable for doctrine, reproof, correction, and instruction in righteousness, that we may be perfect and thoroughly furnished unto all good works. 2nd Timothy 2:15 advises us to study to show ourselves approved, a workman that need not be ashamed, rightly dividing the word of truth. With all I have experienced over the years there's no way I could leave my trust in any of the establishments in this system. The medical field, schools, and even the church are full of deceptions, and that list grows with understanding and acknowledgment of the truth!

Against the doctor's dire warnings, I neglected the medications and removed myself from the facility altogether, never seeing a doctor since now, 7 years later. All I did was change my diet and I recommend everyone address their diet as early as possible for a host of reasons. The dietary law found in Leviticus is a great start. Remember the same creator who created this world created this body and this Law. We know that he does not change, and there is nothing new under the sun. From then and until now I have found that what has been accepted by humanity goes against the guidelines of our Father who art in Heaven. Since we have been warned that Satan is the prince of this dark, deceitful world it should be of no surprise that his guidelines be the ones followed and highlighted. The only way to be set apart is to find our Father in His words, be obedient, and be a light to this final generation.

Psalms 139:14 says, *I will praise you for I am fearfully and wonderfully made: marvelous are your works; and that my soul knows right well."* This verse insinuates how TMH was personally involved in my birth, therefore I trust Him that my body retains all tools necessary to fight all diseases and ailments that I can encounter as long as I live the way he clarified. For this reason, no vaccines or such for me.

3 THE MOST HIGH

"Let us hear the conclusion of the whole matter. Fear Elohiym and keep his commandments for this is the whole duty of man." (Ecc 12:13)

MANY GODS HAVE BEEN created and extolled by man; Psalms 96:4-5 says that TMH (The Most High) is "great and greatly to be praised: He is to be feared above all gods. For all the gods of the nations are idols but [TMH] made the heavens." We must be careful with anything we give our love, power, or respect to, as it becomes our headship and, therefore, our leader. Satan has been running to and from across the world for thousands of years, seeking to deceive the masses into the lake of fire where he is headed soon. This is nothing new, for he has retained thousands of years' worth of deceptions, and he will deceive you if you are not in tune with TMH and His truths. Know for certain that TMH can destroy him at any moment, but that will take place in His timing. As the greatest author and creator of anything ever, His story will happen just as orchestrated. Warning, there is an eternal life vast approaching, and based on your choices today you will be an eternal citizen at the proper dwelling place. It could be heaven where it is said, Eye has not seen, nor ear heard, nor have entered the heart of man the things which TMH has prepared for those who love him. Look, see and understand in its entirety what it's saying throughout the bible, "those who love Me keep My commandments." I find this ultimately important and we will focus on this in the following paragraphs! Regarding hell it is said, they will be thrown into a furnace of fire; and in that place will be weeping, moaning, and gnashing of teeth! TMH has given you free will to follow Him and righteousness or Satan and deceit but know for certain that you will be accountable for your decisions and even lack thereof. Many sources today lie for money, self-glorification, hate, and deception; and the more you understand, the more you will see this. The KJV Bible is the most printed and sold book ever, and although it is not perfect, for Satan and his minions have made prophesied changes, it is holy and adequate for the job. I highly recommend reading the Cepher Bible which is a comprehensive restoration of scripture written in the English language retaining much of the names, etc. that were removed from the modern KJV, if you get the opportunity.

Do not be dismayed, for TMH acknowledged these lies years ago within His Holy Bible. Be encouraged, for He said His sheep hear His voice, and be faithful in knowing that if you seek Him wholeheartedly, He will make His presence known to you. 2 Timothy 1:7 says, "[He] did not give us the spirit of fear but of love, power, and of a sound mind." Allow His Spirit to give you the peace that passes all understanding because this is where you'll find true freedom! Please understand that everything existing is intentional and happens as TMH directs for He is omnipotent(almighty), omniscient(all-knowing), and omnipresent (present everywhere always). The fact that His scrolls written thousands of years ago manifested this Bible that has sold billions of copies today is amazing and is just another sign of His power—as is the fact that the book is still relevant and revealing itself today. Know that we cannot understand the Book based on someone else's point of view because others may have their own agenda or could simply be misled themselves. You must humble yourself and seek His voice, for those that hunger and thirst for righteousness shall be filled. (Matthew 5:6).

James 2:14 says that faith without works is dead. Abraham had work to do when he thought he was sacrificing his son Isaac before TMH provided the lamb. Noah also had to work when TMH told him (against all the sense of the world) to build the ark ahead of the flood. We must always grow and know there is more to learn and do. The Bible says in Matthew 23:11 that the greatest among men is servant of all, so we should serve one another joyfully as if heaven has a bank account attached. I seek to build my riches in heaven where thieves cannot steal nor rust corrupt, and I hope you will stand beside me. To have a chance to make it into heaven's gates, you must familiarize yourself with our Father in heaven and make yourself known to Him.

In Matthew 7:21-23, the Messiah said:

> Not every one that saith unto me, Master, Master, shall enter the Kingdom of heaven; but he that doeth the will of my Father which is in heaven. Many will say in that day, Lord, Lord have we not prophesied in thy name? and in thy name have cast out devils? and in thy name done many wonderful works? And then will I profess unto them, I never knew you: depart from me, ye that work iniquity.

We will all stand before the Judge when all is revealed, and hearing *"depart from me, I never knew you"* will be the worst thing ever because there will be no chances left. Here, the Messiah mandates that we keep the will of His father. TMH gave us ten commandments in Exodus intended for us to keep wholeheartedly, until the end, to show our devotion to Him. Those that TMH sends away He calls workers of iniquity. The dictionary defines iniquity as "immoral or grossly unfair behavior," which is obviously unacceptably bad. The Bible concordance, however, simply defines iniquity as lawlessness or transgressing Torah (which is the first five books of the Bible revealing law)—somehow, someway, we all fall short by this definition. To live righteously is worth living for so much, that it is worth dying for, and I'll give my life in a heartbeat for His cause. Please follow along as I bring a few questions about following our father to your attention.

Again, the Bible clearly states that the devil will transform himself into an angel of light and deceive the world. Sorry for the repetition, but I need you to comprehend this! For this reason, we must be in tune with TMH's establishments and separate from the world to have hope for eternal life. John 4:23 says, "But the hour cometh, and now is when the true worshippers shall worship the Father in spirit and in truth: for the Father seeketh such to worship him." Loved ones please read the Bible without worldly interpretation, seek the truth, and see that TMH did not establish a religion, code, or secrets—2nd Peter 1:20 says, know this that no prophecy of the scripture is of private interpretation. When you look, you will see that He established a nation in Exodus and made a covenant with that nation. In doing so, He established the way of life that needed to be kept until heaven and Earth subsided for us to have a chance at everlasting life. The covenant was made for Israel, but Jeremiah 12:16-17 says, "it shall come to pass, if they will diligently learn the ways of my people to swear by my name, YAH liveth; as they taught my people to swear by Baal; then shall they be built in the midst of my people.

But if they will not obey, I will utterly pluck up and destroy that nation, saith [TMH]." This means that anyone who wholeheartedly follows TMH's laws can find a place in the kingdom. I must strongly highlight and reference the fact that TMH's single, and Holy name today can only be found in the book of Psalms written by King David, who we were also told was the man after His heart. In Psalms 68:4 David told us to sing praises to His name, and extol Him who rideth upon the heavens by His name, YAH! We will discuss the importance of His name and acknowledge some of the pagan titles we've been deceived within the following paragraphs as well. In reference to the image of TMH Revelations 4:3 says, *he was to look upon like a Jasper and Sardine stone.* Which is obviously a dark brown to reddish colored being. The Bible states that the people of every nation will make it through the gates of heaven! Likely, the most important thing I will ever do in my little meek life is to share these next few pages with you, brothers and sisters, and I vow to do my best to give you all of the necessities I can in as few words as possible to make the base foundation clear.

4 BY HIS NAME

"Neither is there salvation in any other for there is no other name under Heaven given among men, whereby we must be saved." (Acts 4:12)

AS A NIGHT OWL, I lie awake nightly reading my Bible, wondering how people are sleeping on these latter-day biblical prophecies manifesting before my eyes. Years ago, I found that the push to follow our dreams was stealing our time and attention. How can we see the bigger picture when we are wholeheartedly focused on our desires? I am certain that TMH YAH did not intend for us to live in this me-against-you or me-above-you world we have come to know, but through the sins of our forefathers, beginning with Adam and Eve, this is today's reality. The world, seeking a share of heaven on Earth, says, "Go for it. It's now or never." I say, "Slow down. Do you want it now or forever?" Even a thousand years of fame and fortune could never compare to eternity, whether it is spent in heaven's joys and beauty or hell's pains and turmoil, so slow down and take heed.

Regardless of your circumstance, the end is drawing near. Turmoil and sorrow are all around us and will only get worse for some time. We must separate from our flesh, portray the characteristics of our Father, and be the light of the world. Television, radio, and especially social media have driven us on the glitz and glamour of this world. We have been blinded by various desires to keep up with or surpass the Joneses. We focus on self-promotion and money instead of the will of TMH YAH and heaven. The truth is that life is not about you or me but the Father and His plan. Again, He gave us free will to decide our path in life, but beware; every individual will stand alone before the Judge when all is revealed, and you will be held accountable.

The scripture is living, and everything prophesied has or is coming true. The world appears to disagree, but just as Revelation 21:9-13 states, "the twelve gates of heaven will hold the names of the twelve tribes of the children of Israel." Read also Ezekiel 20:32-38 and Isaiah 14:1-2 for further proof. The evidence of His power is revealed in His word. It is consistent, it doesn't change, and although it is ridiculed it will accomplish all He has said because He doesn't change. This pandemic resulting from coronavirus or the 5G towers (depending on who you talk to), is opening many eyes, and the world as we know it is experiencing shifts welcoming an entirely new generation. I understand this to be nothing more or less than YAH beginning the plagues as He did before Israel was freed from Egypt. Over time, it will only get worse before the Messiah returns and makes it right once and for all. As written, with a mighty hand, a stretched-out arm, and a pouring fury, YAH will demand the leaders of the world to send His people off again. Unlike in Egypt, His people, the apple of his eye, have now been enslaved and scattered to the four corners of the world, and everyone breathing will witness His almighty power sooner than later. Almost all nations have experienced tribulation to a certain degree, but the specifics of Deuteronomy 28 are still sure today and certainly reveal who His true nation is. I may be jumping the gun a bit on how and when this world we previously knew will come to an end, for I am not a prophet. I just read the same book. I'm hoping you do the same; I am watching His words unfold, and I fully trust the ending where a remnant is redeemed. I'm half Caucasian, and if that means I must be grafted in to be amongst the family, I'll do everything I can. Thankfully, I have faith my mom, a full Caucasian woman, has similar feelings. As written, there will be people of every nation that make it, but sadly only one-third of Israel itself will make it through the heavenly gates. Regardless of your ethnicity or the color of your skin, it is simply about you being obedient to our father who art in heaven! Remember Samuel 15:22 makes that obedience is greater than any sacrifice!

"Fear YAH and keep His commandments: for this is the whole duty of man" (Ecclesiastes 12:13). This eternal pledge of allegiance has not changed. King Solomon the son of king David, and the wisest man ever, also said in Proverbs 9:10 that the fear of YAH is the beginning of wisdom and the knowledge of the holy is understanding. If your worldly dad makes a command, you fear the repercussions when you fall short of the demand. How much more than with our heavenly Father?

Though scripture insinuates that there are many gods, the El (mighty one) of Abraham, Isaac, and Jacob has a holy Name, YHWH. King David, the man after YHWH's heart told us in Psalms 68:4, to extol Him by His name YAH, giving us a free-of-excuse, single-syllable verification. As the creator of everything YAH deserves maximum reverence! The least we can do as His children is call Him by His set apart name, which is found in His universal praise, HalleluYAH, meaning praise YAH. Yes, there are existing terms that bear some qualities that He possesses like almighty, king of kings, and the most-high, to name a few; however, not one of those titles hold the holy factor of YHWH, meaning "self-existing one," for no other being could ever make this claim, Holy.

I encourage, and even beg you to research the names we have been led to call YAH. Again, beware for the deceiver is working overtime to trick the world as the end draws near. Why when I research the name Lord do, I find it was synonymous with the name of the false god Baal who was worshipped by the Canaanites in the beginning. Look for yourself, there are many scriptures like Hosea 2:16-17 warning that many of us will be extolling the names of Baal again towards the end. I never heard anyone praise or even utter the name Baal, but my research has proven for me that lord was a synonymous name for baal. Think about this and understand that any translations existing today are of man (at best), and much of it will have deceptive roots since Satan has been running to and fro with these deceptions for all these years, take it serious, pray and do research. Satan again is father of lies and prince on earth so it should be of no surprise that the names of false gods would be titles for our creator in these last days, deception!!

Terry Macalmon wrote a song that says, "I sing praises to your name, oh Lord, praises to your name, oh Lord." The song continues with "for your name is great and greatly to be praised." For years, I thought that song and a few others baring "Lord" were beautiful, but I now see that, just as prophesied, most of our leaders have been deceived or, even worse, sold out and we must search for this truth ourselves. I recall watching *Jeopardy!* years ago with my dad. The question was, "Who is the Canaanite God whose name means lord?" Alex Trebek's answer was "Baal." My spirit was shook, leading me to further research and prove. I also used to call TMH YAH, God for the first 25 years of my life, but the Book of Enoch—that is mentioned in but since removed from the Bible—declares that the fallen angel who beguiled Eve with the fruit was named Gadreel (pronounced god-rael). The names appear too similar, so I question the root of this word, which is not His name and a powerless new age title at best. The Bible, when searched through, tells us His name again in Psalms 68:4 and you must understand how important His name is, which is why the deceptive translators in this system went through all the trouble to have the name all but removed placing his name in vain to the masses. We have widely accepted these other titles and names created by men or likely worse. These titles and names are lackadaisical and deceitful; if you think I am wrong do some research on the beloved name Jesus we've been given as representation for the name of the Messiah. Earth pig, and hail Zeus will be common outcomes. I have had this exact conversation with countless pastors; although they do not have a clear answer for the foundation from which these names or titles come and have been accepted, they then acknowledge they are not His original name, yet they are upset when I refuse to use them. Check out the names of the prophets; for many of them held YAH's name within their name—ObadiYAH, meaning servant of YAH; JeremiYAH, meaning YAH will rise; and JosiYAH, meaning founded of YAH to name a few, but their names represent their duty to YAH. Do not be fooled by our language; we are looking for the YAH sound, but the spelling is often twisted.

    I must also expound that the Messiah (MessiYAH as my dad says) came in His Father's name, YAHusha, meaning YAH's salvation. Acts

4:12 says, "Neither is there salvation in any other: for there is none other name under heaven given among men, whereby we must be saved." We must be grounded in this understanding and be leaders and not followers. In John 5:43, YAHshua said, "I am come in my Father's name, and ye receive me not: if another shall come in his own name, him will you receive." Where did the name "Jesus" come from? According to my research, it is no secret that the letter J did not even exist 500 years ago, let alone the 2,000 years ago when the Messiah walked the earth. My 1611 KJV Bible does not bear the J at all. Most importantly, one name means one name, and it is foolish to believe these worldly interpretations are the work of YAH. Again, we must separate ourselves from this world!

If this is not enough to get your attention, let us look at another verse very commonly used in the church. John 3:16 says, "For YAH so loved the world, that he gave his only begotten son, that whosoever believes in him should not perish, but have everlasting life." I grew up hearing and loving that verse daily, but two verses down in John 3:18 says, "For [YAH] sent not his son into the world to condemn the world; but that the world through Him may be saved. He that believes on Him is not condemned: but he that believeth not is condemned already, because he hath not believed in the NAME of the only begotten Son of YAH." I had grandparents who were very involved in the church, had a strong relation to the name of Jesus, and likely never heard the name YAHusha because they passed before this truth was revealed. Thankfully, they had a strong desire for righteousness as well, and as Acts 17:30 insinuates, I have faith that YAH winked at this ignorance, knowing His name would be altered in this final captivity, and He will weigh all hearts in judgment. Continuing in John 5:41-44 messiah says, "I receive no honor from men. But I know you, that you have not the love of YAH in you. I come in my father's name, and you receive me not: if another shall come in his own name, him you will receive. How can ye believe, which receive honor one of another, and seek not the honor that cometh from YAH only." I cry for us to seek this truth because it is now at our fingertips and He was most aware of the internet and google even before the foundation of the world. He told us He is looking for us to worship in spirit and truth; if you decide not to honor this, you will be held accountable, and you cannot blame anyone, for we have also been told throughout the book to seek him while He may be found.

Colossians 2:8 prophesied that we would be addicted to the traditions of our dads instead of abiding by YAH's law, making the word of YAH of no effect through the traditions we deliver. I have a large family who still call themselves Christians, but I pray they understand that Jesus is a new name and YAH will not share His glory with another. Understand that YAH and YAHusha are the names the deceiver hates. He and his minions have worked nonstop to remove these names from existence for too many years, but YAH, the author of everything, has left many clues for his children who care to seek Him out. If you care for truth, seek it and you will find Him. If you decide His name does not matter and you can call Him whatever they translate next, beware for He is Holy. We now have many sources proving, without a doubt, the prophesied tricks that have been pushed on us for years; if you care for the truth, seek it!

5 THE COVENANT

"And it shall come to pass, if they will diligently learn the ways of my people, to swear by name, YAHUAH lives; as they taught my people to swear to by Ba'al; then shall they be built in the midst of my people...But they will not obey, I will utterly pluck up and destroy that nation, says YAHUAH."
(Jeremiah 12: 16 & 17)

MY ANCESTORS WERE AT FAULT in the first place for breaking the covenant as forewarned, but the truth is coming into the light in these latter days as prophesied, and it is our responsibility to pick up the pieces, observe the covenant, and show the world. Again, the letter J is not even five hundred years old, and our faith must lie where the evidence is heaviest. In the 1611 KJV Bible, there isn't a single J, so naturally, the name Jesus, which is not a Hebrew name, did not exist. If you care for truth, ask then, who on Earth dares to translate Holy? A name change was recorded when Jacob was renamed Israel; and this happened multiple times within scripture. How then can this so-called translation be accepted, especially when we were forewarned that ONLY ONE name was given for our redemption and this was before the J existed? Who is the authority for this translation? Do we not take our Father for His word? Did He not know they would distort this name? YAH forbid, therefore YAH told us to seek Him. There will be no excuse for the disrespect or even carelessness when we go before the Judge. If He was changing the very name given for redemption, He would have clearly said it in the scriptures. When and how did this translation become holy and therefore fit the bill? I would love for anyone who disagrees to bring forth facts, and we can search the scriptures out together.

I am sure I will ruffle feathers with this, and if that is what it takes to arouse the conversation, I am all for it. Luke 12:2 verifies that everything being done in darkness would be brought into the light. Luke 15:7 also speaks of all of heaven rejoicing when a single soul transforms from the deceptive matrix system, so to speak, into the simple light of truth. Wide and broad is the gate to destruction, thankfully, there is a narrow road to life, though few will find it (Matthew 7:13). Satan again transforms himself into an angel of light, and deceives the world, and just as the Christmas holiday is truly deceptive (former baby sacrifices, modern covetousness, etc.), I find no validity in the name Christ. Messiah means anointed of YAH, but Christ simply means anointed, but of whom? The only Christ I've known is Jesus who I've found to be a lie, so it appears Satan is deceiving again? If you find otherwise as a believer, I hold you accountable to bring forth facts to me. You can simply look up Old Nick, also known as Santa, in the dictionary and find that the definition is Satan himself. Jeremiah 10:3-6 shows that the celebration of Christmas is spiritual adultery, as are all holidays, also known as new world holy days. They have no reference in the scripture, and as you depart from the masses, you'll see them for the hell of days they truly are. The weekly seventh day of rest, known as the Sabbath, is the only significant day YAH left us with until His son returns, and His kingdom is restored. The ancient holy days have been left as signals, but that is for in-depth studies.

These different religions, most of which have a place in the coexist symbol overly present on vehicles today, are accepted by the world and Satan himself. Remember YAH told us to be in the world but not of this world. Yet, we clearly see the world trying to coexist by all means necessary. Again, James 4:4 says that a friend of the world is an enemy of YAH, so keep in mind that you must separate yourself from the masses. Please read 2nd Thessalonians 2 which speaks of that mystery of iniquity and a strong delusion sent to the world that they would believe a lie, and they would be damned who believed not the simple truth of old! 2nd Thesolonians 2:15 says *"Therefore brethren stand fast, and keep the commandment which you have been taught whether by word or Cepher."* The church sounds and even at times feels good, but it is a whoredom; in Revelation 18:4 YAH recommended that we "come out of her " that we be not partakers of her sins and receive not of her plagues. 2nd Corinithians 14:14 says Satan disguises himself as an angel of light and what better way for him to do that then become part of the church. As said before YAH gave us one single way to heaven, and the kings of the world have all presented and represented the religions that alter what YAH has mandated in various ways! He will not share His esteem (glory) with any other! Rev 17:2 mentions the whore with whom the kings of the earth committed fornication, and the inhabitants of the earth have been made drunk with the wine of her fornication. In Rev 17:17 it says Yah put in their head to give their kingdom to the beast, it all started with one major religion and they are still in position today. All of religion is spiritual adultery, and I recall my sister, a nurse, jokingly saying people need a cranial-rectal-ectomy! In all seriousness, the truth is there, but people want to follow the masses and be hand-fed instead of seeking and applying truth for themselves. My pleasure and duty in life is honoring my Father YAH, and it brings me immense joy to fellowship with heaven-seekers. If I can contribute to a heavenly cheer even once, I can die peacefully.

Scripture says our self-righteousness is as filthy rags, which is why I would like to remind us all to repent daily. We were born in sin, and again, all fall short. The idea is to be a set-apart light to a generation of lost, wandering souls. There is no code, secret, or riches that will get you through the gates of heaven. It is also not about being lucky enough to be free of sin when the Messiah returns. Practicing righteousness must be a way of life! This entire life on Earth is as vapor—it evaporates so fast as a test for our eternal dwelling place. The KJV Bible, the most printed and sold book of all time, tells us just how to accomplish this on the blessed end. In Exodus 20, YAH wrote with his own finger ten commandments for His chosen people, the Israelites (Studies show they were called Y'sraelites, for His nation also held His name. [Jeremiah 14:9]), after they left Egypt. He further proclaimed the commandments were to be kept until heaven and Earth subsided (Matthew 5:18). Revelation 22:14, the very last chapter of the entire bible says, "Blessed are they that keep the commandments that they may have rite the tree of life." 1 John 2:3-4 says, "And hereby we do know that we know Him, if we keep His commandments. He that saith, I know Him, and keep not His commandments, is a liar, and the truth is not in him."

YAHusha, our savior and Messiah, told us in John 14:15, "If you love me, keep my command-ments." When the rich young ruler asked the Messiah what good thing to do to have eternal life, YAHusha said that to have life, he must keep the commandments. In Luke 10:25-28, when the lawyer asked what the greatest commandment was, YAHusha in his competence replied, "Thou shalt love [YAH] your

[Elohim] with all your heart, soul, mind, and strength; and thy neighbor as thyself," those two acts fulfill the whole law and the prophets. Raised a Christian for the first 20 years of my life, I was convinced that the commandments went null and void with the Messiah's ultimate sacrifice. However, as I grew in my studies over the years, I saw that YAHusha prophesied against this very thought in Matthew 5:17-19 where he said:

> Think not that I came to abolish the law or the prophets. I did not come to destroy but to fulfill for verily I say unto you till heaven and earth pass not one jot or tittle will pass from the law, till all be fulfilled. Therefore if any man break the least of these commandments and teach others also, they shall be called the least in the kingdom, and if any man do the least of these commandments and teach others they shall be called great in the kingdom.

In that sermon on the mount, we find all ten commandments in that one perfect sentence. Commandments Five through Ten can be summed up as loving your neighbor as yourself, but I will write them for you to judge. Then, I will go through how Commandments One through Four show that we are to wholeheartedly love YAH and give him headship.

6 THE COMMANDMENTS

"For this is the love of YAH, that we guard his commandments; and his commandments are not grievous."
(1st John 5:3)

COMMANDMENT FIVE SAYS, "Honor thy father and thy mother: that thy days may be long upon the land which YAH thy Elohim giveth thee." Six says, "Thou shalt not kill." Seven says, "Thou shalt not commit adultery." Eight says, "Thou shalt not steal." Nine says, "Thou shalt not bear false witness against thy neighbor." Ten says, "Thou shalt not covet anything that is your neighbor's." If we followed these commandments, the world would be a peaceful place, but as mere humans, most, if not all, of us fall short in just these six commandments. James 2:10 tells us that offending even just one commandment is like breaking them all. Just to be clear, James is not talking about someone making a mistake and breaking a commandment, for again we all fall short and our duty is to acknowledge, repent, and seek improvement. James is talking about people deciding, for whatever reason, not to honor a commandment, for this will not be tolerated. Sadly, I find major folly, deception, and hypocrisy in the teaching of Commandments One through Four, and I will take the next few paragraphs to expound because this is the focus of this book.

These first four commandments are like YAH's seal and show a direct allegiance to Him. A corporate seal contains the name, date, and state of incorporation—maybe you will find a resemblance. I cannot stress enough that you must separate from this world and get in tune with YAH in His word because so much has been done to belittle the importance of these commandments. The belittling is especially true for these first four commands, even though we were told just seven verses from the end of the book, in Revelation 22:14, "Blessed are they that do his commandments, that they may have right to the tree of life, and may enter in through the gates into the city." To seal something means to join two things to prevent them from coming apart or from anything passing between them. That is the relationship with YAH we all should be seeking. Numbers 23:19 states that YAH is not a man that he should lie or the son of man that he should change his mind. This is one of many verses in scripture that make clear that YAH does not change; even when I went to church, I believed this, so I always had questions about the belittled commandments. Again, Matthew 5:18 says, "Till heaven and earth pass, one jot or one tittle shall in no way pass from the law till all be fulfilled." That is exactly what it sounds like. YAH means what He says, and just as Isaiah 56:11 prophecies, His word will not return to Him void and will accomplish all that He has said.

When studying the Bible precept upon precept you will see it clearly states that if you love YAH, you will wholeheartedly keep His commandments. Therefore in faith, you trust Him with all details of your existence, knowing nothing gets by Him. It is written from the first book (Abraham kept the commandments) through the last book that YAHusha kept the commandments, as did the disciples after YAHusha sacrificed His life. Many Christians quote Paul from Colossians 2:14-17 when rebuking this stance, but keep in mind that the Mosaic Law was written by the hand of Moses being referenced in this reference. Yes all of these principles written by Moses were righteous from the beginning but when the veil was torn when Messiah was crucified. The only laws that were to be in your heart and read are the 10 commandments written by Yah's finger. There were other Sabbath's day of intermission besides that Holy 7th day. Read Deuteronomy 31:9-13, and what was separate from 10 Commandments for further verification. Paul clarifies in Roman 6:15 saying, "shall we sin because we are not under the law? YAH forbid. Contrary to this stance is the fact that the Ten Commandments were written by YAH's finger (see Exodus 25:16, 21-22 and Exodus 31:18), and the Ark was built to house them within because Moses broke them once before, yet they were to last forever. Moses's handwritten laws were placed beside the

Ark, representing that they were temporary. The whole law of Torah was/is righteous and should be acknowledged for health and righteousness.

Commandment One states, "Thou shalt have no other gods before me." As a Christian, I figured I had this covered 100 percent because I was raised in the Father, the Son, and the Holy Spirit and never knew or acknowledged other deities. I found that the rich young ruler was also familiar with the gospel and responded to keeping the commandments religiously as the Messiah quoted a few. Seeing deeper into the young man's heart, the Messiah told the rich young ruler to sell all he had, give to the poor, and follow Him, but the rich young ruler could not abide and left. YAHusha then told the disciples in Matthew 19:24 that it was easier for the camel to make it into the eye of the needle than for a rich man to make it into heaven. This is not because money is evil, but the love of money is the root of all evil, as Timothy 6:10 states. Loved ones, reaching overtime for money, fame, or accolades will eventually lead to your demise when they become your heaven on Earth. Begin living for forever by giving all praise and headship to our creator YAH, who is also the one and only father (Matthew 23:9)! He must be your first and last thought in everything for a chance in the kingdom. Nothing and no one can be closer or more important to you than He is. Everything here is temporal treasure, compared to eternity there's no measure, the only true reward is in heaven, proceed with caution, do you want it now or do you want it forever. You cannot serve two masters (Mathew 6:24), and a little leaven leavens the whole lump (Galatians 5:9).

Commandment Two says:

> Thou shalt not make unto thee any graven image, or any likeness of anything that is in heaven above, or that is in the earth beneath, or that is in the water under the earth: thou shalt not bow down thyself, nor serve them: for I YAH thy El am a jealous El, visiting the iniquity of the fathers upon the children unto the third and fourth generation of them that hate me, and showing mercy unto thousands of them that love me and keep my commandments.

I looked up "graven image" and found it to be any carved idol, usually wood or stone, used as an object of worship. Flabbergasted, I recall at the head of the churches I attended was a cross—this weapon usually carved in wood, which was used to mock, murder, and torture countless humans as well as the Messiah himself. I repent again for my ignorance as a boy bowing before the cross at the head of the church, seeking His presence. The mockery continues, as I find this image as the charm to countless necklaces around the world, and even though we are told not to ink our bodies, I have countless friends and family members paying money to have that cross tattooed on a bicep or back. I know we were told in Luke 14:27 to bear our own cross, but that refers to the difficulties of this life, especially when Satan sees a threat in you and continuing to verse 33 He says you must forsake all that you have to be a disciple. Instead of a cross I envision a crossroads, and a place of decisions. According to Acts 5:30, Acts 13:29, and 1st Peter 2:24 it was a tree. Galatians 3:13 even gives overwhelming prophetic implication that he was hung on a tree you can understand when it says in the Cepher it writes, "Messiah, has redeemed us from the curse of Torah being made a curse for us: for it is written, cursed is everyone that hangs on a tree." Many of my ancestors were hung on trees as well. You won't have to search very far to find this symbol of the cross that was formerly the mark of Tamuz thousands of years before Messiah. The cross can be found all around the world, and ever-present on the hieroglyphics found in the pyramids of Egypt.

We don't need a church building, for we are living stones ourselves and as Acts 7:48 says, *YAH dwelleth not in temples made with the hands of men.* We need to come together to edify one another, and anywhere two or more are gathered in His name, He is in the midst. We must seek YAH and His direction all day every day. That graven image is of powerless deceit. Nowhere in scripture do we find a disciple, a prophet, or any believer wearing or bowing to a cross. Ask your teacher or pastor where this began and where the scripture appointed this image as holy or acceptable.

Remember, when we meet the Judge, only how we followed HIM and His directions will matter. Obedience is greater than sacrifice, and we must thoughtfully inspect everything in which we partake. Satan is prince of this deceitful world, but YAH warned us about the tricks he would use to lead us to hell with him.

We were told to make no image, but we have this image of Christ with straight hair usually hovered by a large sun. The scripture took the time to say Messiah had hair like wool and copper skin which could be any color of a penny. Again, if you do a little research, you will find this picture of Jesus Christ to be none other than Caesar Borgia, the son of a pope. A dear Friend and lover of Leonardo da Vinci!! Who created the picture we still use for Christ today. The definition of Christ is anointed, but I ask again, anointed by whom? Messiah (or MessiYAH, as my dad says) in Hebrew means anointed of YAH (holy), and the more I study, the more I find Satan introducing false names, narratives, and deceptions galore. My desire is for you to seek this information for yourself and realize how much we've been deceived, and how much Satan has held on the world today. Again, YAH seeks those who will worship Him in spirit and in truth.

Continuing with the importance of His Name, Commandment Three states, "Thou shalt not take the name of [YAH] thy [El] in vain for [YAH] will not hold him guiltless that taketh His name in vain." Again, as a Christian, I thought this meant not to say things like "goddammit" or "I promise to god," but it does not. First, the word god is not a name but a title! Remember, the Bible tells us there are many gods (1 Corinthians 8:5). Second, vain means useless, pointless, or outdated. In other words, not using His holy name of YAH, which is singular, is taking His name in vain. Again, King David, the man after YAH's heart, told us in Psalms 68:4 to extol Him by His Name YAH! YHWH, YAHWEH, YAHUAH, all bear that name, which means self-existing one, meets the holy factor. This is the name the Sadducees and Pharisees banned from the disciples and the same name removed from the entire scripture barring King David's book. Who dares to translate holy? Titles exist that speak of who He is like Alpha (beginning) and Omega (end), as well as Almighty and Most High, but these are not His name. How often does the scripture speak of YAH doing things for His Name's sake?

Satan has deceived the world, and as the angel of light he was said to be in 2 Corinthians 11:14, he does not need to turn you into a murderer or even a thief—he simply needs you to transgress YAH's law and the testament of YAHusha. 2 Corinthians 11:15 also speaks of Satan's ministers becoming as ministers of righteousness furthering the deceptions. Regardless of what you've been told, YAH's name is the most important name ever, and as the only self-existing being, HE is omnipotent (all-powerful), omniscient (all-knowing), and omnipresent (present everywhere, always), we need not question anything

He has ordained! Everything was recorded before the foundation of the world, and everything He and the prophets have said will play out accordingly. Who is the one that decided these other names fit the bill because unless YAH said it, it is a lie! Read the Book for yourself, and extol Him by His name YAH!! Powerful!

With all the deception, and lack of care to search out the truth, it's no wonder such a small number finds eternal life. It must be of utmost importance for you to find Him! Names are not to be translated! How much sense does it make, then, to translate the name of the Creator and His son the Messiah, especially when He plainly said His Son's Name is the only name given by which we can be saved? (Acts 4:12) Is it not the most important thing to seek out this single Name for you salvation depends on it. YAH's son came in His name, and evidence suggests they (the leaders of this world) have a perpetual hate for this name and want it removed altogether. Rev 17:17 says YAH put in their head to give their kingdom to the beast. Read also Psalms 83:1-8 which speaks of kings of the world taking crafty counsel to cut them from being a nation that the name of Ysrael would be forgotten.

The first recorded use of the name Jesus began as a ship called "Jesus of Lubeck." This became the first slave ship in the 1600's by the British. When broken down this name is Pagan and carries so much deception. YAH is not about confusion, and He was most credible.The church as a business understands and takes advantage of the fact that the human brain seeks visual love and acceptance as opposed to truth and obedience. This is spiritual warfare and much bigger than any individual and is one of Satan's tricks. Again, in Revelation 18 HE urged His people to come out of her, (the world, and this includes all religious establishments) that you be not partakers of her sins and receive not of her plagues. Do not think I am saying everyone within the church is playing a part in the deceit; I am saying the church itself is one of Satan's traps and on a spiritual level this is where all religions fail and fall. Revelations 17:2 says "the kings of the earth have committed fornication with Babylon the great, the mother of all harlots, and the abomination of the earth (Esau, Edom, Jews, Catholic church, Rome) and you can simply read the book of Obadiah,(one chapter) to see their demise. This means that they have agreed to go against YAH, who already verified there is only one true faith. Jeremiah 12:16&17 speaks of the birthing of these religions which push us to call Him by these pagan names of Baal, and celebrate their pagan holidays. This is too deep and hopefully one day we can discuss how this was done and by whom.

    As I said before, the title "Lord" is the surname of the Canaanite deity Baal. Hosea 2:17 says, "For I will take the names of Baalim out of her mouth, and they shall no more be remembered by name." If you still think it is okay to call YAH Lord, why does He speak in Hosea 2:14-17 of believers no longer calling him

Baal but Ishi (husband)? Also, Jeremiah 12:16-17 says, "It shall come to pass that if they will diligently learn the ways of my people to swear by my name, YAH liveth; as they taught my people to swear by Baal (lord); then they shall be built in the midst of my people. But if they will not obey, I will utterly pluck up and destroy that nation." The covenant is for Israel, but the commands are for every heaven-seeker. Heaven is open to anyone, but you must familiarize yourself with Him, His word, and especially the Ten commandments. Unfortunately for most going to church will not accomplish this. Jeremiah 23:25-27 says:

> I have heard what the prophets said that prophesy lies in my name saying I have dreamed. How long shall this be in the heart of prophets that prophesy lies? Yes, they are prophets of the deceit of their own heart; which think to cause my people to forget my name by their dreams which they tell every man to his neighbor as their fathers forgot my name for Baal.

Beware and don't follow a pastor or anyone else; you must have, and seek a personal relationship with YAH for yourself.

Commandment Four says:

> Remember the Sabbath day to keep it holy. Six days shalt thy labor, and do all

> thy work: But the seventh day is the Sabbath of the Most High Elohim: In it thou shalt not do any work, thou nor thy son, nor thy daughter, thy manservant, nor thy maidservant, nor thy cattle, nor thy stranger that is within your gates: For in six days YAH made heaven and earth, the sea, and all that in them is, and rested the seventh day: wherefore YAH blessed the Sabbath day, and hallowed it consecrated and honored.

We know Saturday is that sacred holy day. The evening and the morning were the first day based on creation in Genesis. With that understanding, when the sun goes down on Friday until the sun goes down Saturday, we are to rest, separate from all things worldly, and meditate on YAH and His word. This set-apart day was established on the seventh day of creation before the introduction of sin, and, as prophesied, it would be a sign between Him and His people forever (Exodus 31:17).

On March 7, 321 AD, well after the Messiah sacrificed his life, Roman emperor Constantine 1st issued a civil decree making Sunday (the first day) the day of rest from labor, stating the people should rest upon the venerable day of the sun(sun worship). Opposing the 7th day of rest marked by YAH! Sadly, many people lost their lives based on that decree at that time, and still today you will find the pope stating the Sunday service to be the church's mark or sign. YAH already clarified and sanctified the 7th day Sabbath/shabbat to be a sign between Him and the children of Y'srael forever, and the only mark I'm familiar with that denounces the words of YAH is the mark of the beast. We should be worshipping YAH every day, but Saturday—the seventh day, the Sabbath day—is holy! For this reason, on this day, we commemorate Him for the creation of everything in existence. He created everything before resting on the seventh day; not because he needed rest, nonsense, He simply took some time to admire and consecrate His work. To honor Him and His creation, we must rest and devote ourselves to Him for all that He's done. It is said in Exodus 31:16 His children shall keep the sabbath, and it will be a perpetual sign and covenant until the end. If you decide to only give attention to and follow what man has accepted to be part of the Bible, note that Daniel 12:4 prophecies of knowledge being increased when books are unsealed in final days. Daniel 7:25 also speaks of the beast who shall speak great words against YAH, and wear out the patience of the saints. He will think to change times and laws (sabbath day etc.) and exhaust His saints!

We do not keep the commandments to have passage into heaven, we keep them because he said those who love Him keep HIS commandments, and we seek to be obedient. The drastic effect the Roman government had when scripture was translated still holds strong in the world today, and it takes much determination and discernment to begin to see the bigger picture. The lies are too common, but, as prophesied, the truth is coming into the light, and the world as we know it is experiencing final shifts. Rome's Council of Nicaea was created in 325 AD, four years after Constantine "changed" the Sabbath day, and they have been controlling the world in scripture through the church ever since. Proverbs 1:5 states, "A wise man will hear and increase learning, and a man of understanding will attain unto wise counsel while the fool despises instruction." If truth, history, and the scriptures support it, there is no argument! I am not claiming to be wise; I am only recommending you seek truth everywhere because I promise lies are surrounding us.

7 TWO NATIONS

"And, behold, I come quickly; and my reward is with me, to give every man according as his work shall be. I am the beginning and the end, the first and the last. Blessed are they that do YAHUAH'S commandments, that they may have right to the tree of life, and may enter in through the gates into the city." (Revelations 22: 12-14)

THE BIBLE from Genesis to Revelation is focused on two nations. Abraham in his righteousness was promised to be the father of YAH's chosen nation. However, he also became the father of many nations in time through other women, leading to confusion. Continuing with the holy seed, which was promised by YAH, Abraham's son Isaac impregnated his wife Rebecca who was experiencing remarkable pains during her pregnancy. She was then given understanding on the matter when YAH told her that there were twins representing two separate nations at war within her belly and revealed the qualities the babies would hold. Malachi 1: 2 & 3 speaks on the fact that Jacob, YAH loves, and Esau he hates. Continuing to verse 6 YAH says A son honors his father and a servant his master. If I am a master, where is my fear for you to despise my name. Later, when Rebecca was in delivery, Jacob was the first to expose himself, as lace was tied around his exposed wrist, but somehow, Esau was the first one delivered. In 2nd Esdras, another book originally in the KJV now held in the Apocrypha, verses 7-9 state, "The sign for the end of this world and the beginning of the next would be Jacob's connected hand to Esau's foot during birth." The last shall be first without gap! The corrupt world today is fueled by lies, hate, and crime with Esau's descendants (the Edomites) leading the way, confused and believing they are Jews (fake Hebrew Israelites, Rev 2:9; 5:9 that say they are jews but are synagogue of Satan). Jacob's seed the Y'sraelites will suddenly lead in righteousness and truth when mystery Babylon falls.

The twins lived full lives before their dad, Isaac, aware his end was near, requested for Esau—who was a hunter, his firstborn, and favorite —to fetch, kill, and cook a proper meal, so he could bless Esau before his final breath. Rebecca heard this and had a proper meal prepared on Jacob's behalf as she dressed her favorite son, Jacob, with fake hair across his body so Isaac, who could hardly see, would confuse Jacob for his hairy older brother Esau and bless him. Just as Rebecca planned and YAH ordained, Jacob received the blessing of his dad. Upon Esau's return, Isaac, with much regret, still mustered prophecy for Esau, written in Genesis 27:36-41. It was established that Esau would eventually rule by the sword, and this is the world we live in today.

Let us explore one of the biggest secrets on Earth that clarifies who Jacob is in the world today. Keep in mind that Egypt means bondage. The entire chapter of Deuteronomy 28 is clear and true, but give your attention to verse 68; For the world knows what happened to the only people enslaved as bondmen and bondwomen by ships to the west. The so-called African Americans in America are truly the tribe of Judah (YAHudah), and some of Benjamin and scripture makes it clear that righteousness will rule the world once they acknowledge the covenant lead Israel from the four corners of the world to its rightful place.

With all due respect, an African American man in any religion is a *'nigger'*. Again, I mean no disrespect; I just hope that statement caught your attention. In love, I do not say that derogatorily; it meant lacking knowledge and remaining ignorant. No wonder the slave masters referred to us as *'niggers'*; they stripped everything we had from us and gave us their story which was lies and not history. If you are a non-believer or spiritually careless, you've established your position, and I will love you from a distance regardless. However, for those who have a desire for heaven and an itch for truth, please read the word for yourself because the Bible says that the prophets of latter days are deceived.

The history regarding these so-called African Americans and all of Israel has been systematically wiped out, and the very troubles African Americans have suffered were pre-ordained in Deuteronomy 28. Due to lack of obedience, the seed of Jacob which was as two sticks (Ezekiel 37:15-28) has been scattered to the four corners of the world, as prophesied. Here in America, we predominantly have the tribe of Yahudah, now called Judah (which is where both King David and YAHusha came from), and some of Benjamin. Around 400 years ago, in 1619, my ancestors were pulled from the slave ships singing kumbaYAH, which was a Hebrew hymn calling for YAH's help. In our ignorance as a stiff-necked people, for thousands of years, we have continually traded our most prestigious nationality for various ties to these religious and worldly whoredoms, which is sadly what got us in trouble with TMH YAH in the first place. He clearly told us to be not of this world but to be transformed by the renewing of our minds. We must decide to unlearn what we have been taught by this deceitful system and relearn based on substance and evidence.

It does not matter what religion you are in because they are all created to pull you from our Father and His single truth. Acknowledging the amazing lengths taken to prevent us from knowing who we are is only a small piece to this prophesied story, and I find more lies continually on a weekly basis. YAH did not establish any religion but a nation. Revelation 21:9-13 says the names on heaven's gates would be of the 12 tribes of Israel, and the only way in those gates is given in the 10

Commandments to follow the guidelines and laws established to those people. Again, read Jeremiah 12:16-17 for further proof. The other ten tribes, representing the other stick of Israel, went into captivity well before Benjamin and Judah, but scripture speaks of the sticks coming together once again, which I am beginning to see today. YAHusha's death did away with the blood laws and priesthood; therefore, no more sacrifices or tithes are necessary, for He was the ultimate unblemished sacrifice. Revelation 14:12 makes it clear that the ones YAH considers His saints are those keeping His commandments and the testimony of YAHusha. In Matthew 11, Yahusha said His yoke was easy, and HIS burden was light; I believe this is because He knew that after his sacrifice, keeping His commandments would be more than doable, considering we no longer would have to trouble ourselves with animal sacrifices and such. He also knew that for those who loved HIM and made HIS purpose their own (through the power of the "HOLY SPIRIT"), keeping HIS commandments and doing the will of the FATHER would be a joy.

Keep seeking Him and make a habit of truly repenting and improving, for there is so much to learn. For example, I initially had difficulty keeping the Sabbath, which after 12 years cost me my job. I began working for myself and as I committed, customers adapted; nowadays, I am sometimes praised for my conviction when passing on big money jobs available on the Sabbath day. Now, I look forward to the Sabbath every week, and as someone who struggled with sleep and general rest for as long as I can remember, the Sabbath day is my delight! For an outline on how to keep it, I recommend reading the Book of Jubilees.

Loved ones, when it is all said and done, you must understand that Satan does not need you to team up with a big bad guy ready to steal, kill, and destroy. As I have said, Satan transforms into an angel of light, and scripture says he will deceive the world. As an illusionist and the author of confusion, he works tirelessly to come up with the next way to trick and make us stumble, for there is only one way to heaven and innumerable ways to keep us out. Again, Ecclesiastes 12:13 says to fear YAH and keep His commandments for this is the full duty of man. The commandments are simply a way of life that verify your allegiance to YAH; the whole law written by Moses pushes you to be a healthy individual inside and out to this day. YAH is unfathomably magnificent, and He knew every detail seen and unseen since before the foundation of the world. There has never been a mistake or surprise for Him. YAHusha Messiah himself said that He did not come to abolish the law or prophets but to fulfill. Keep the commandments and seek a personal relationship with YAH.

AFTERWORD

IF YOU HUNGER FOR TRUTH, apply understanding and connect Deuteronomy 28 (with close attention to verse 68) and Zechariah 8:23! In Luke 13:27, the masses who show up for judgment proclaim that they have done great works in YAH's name. YAH responds with "I know you not; depart from me you workers of iniquity," which simply means transgressors of the law. The law was wrapped up in the ten commandments, and that is all you need to be guilty of breaking to dishonor TMHt! The powers that be are under YHWH's control. YAH has ordained, and none will return to Him void. When He said one Name was given by which we can be saved, it refutes man's decision to translate the holy name that Satan wants deleted and forgotten. If you still find the single name of righteousness to be unimportant, please see John 1:11-12, which says, "He came unto his own and his own received Him not. But as many as received Him, to them gave He power to become the sons of [YAH], even to them that believe in His NAME!" Again, read John 3:18— two verses after the church's most famous scripture— that says, "He that believes on Him is not condemned: but he that believeth not is condemned already, because he hath not believed in the NAME of the only begotten son of YAH!"

As I touched on earlier, the letter J was not created until 1524 AD. It is YAH's work in having man choose to translate His son's name into a name that couldn't have existed, for He knew this information would be readily available toward the end of days. YAHusha is holy and sacred. Jesus is a manmade tradition by one of the new age languages frowned upon in scripture! We must have a heart of clay and choose not to remain a stone on the fact that a foreign deity was delivered to us in replacement of MessiYAH in the JC character. We have blasphemed the holy name of our father almighty YAHUAH. We must have a true desire to praise, glorify, and amplify His holy Name of YAH. Look at how much effort, disrespect, and deceit has been portrayed and even enforced in the lengthy process of removing His name from our everyday vocabulary. We simply are not following His word, but it was prophesied that in the last days, man will not endure sound doctrine. Perilous times are coming. Seek Him wholeheartedly without doubt. We must also be sharing this with the next generation. I have no children but spend time with nieces and nephews, and sadly I find today that these kids only desire entertainment which is alarming.

I find it interesting that Revelation 12:17 says that the dragon (which is Satan) is wroth with the woman that gave birth to the man-child (Yahusha) and went to make war with her seed, the Hebrew

Israelites, that guard the commandments of YAH and the testimony of Yahusha MessiYAH. Although the world seems to be shifting in our favor, Ezekiel 20:32-38 proclaims that no matter how many times Israel tries, they will not be accepted as another family of the countries of this world serving wood and stone, so stay on your toes and in your Bible, family. The love of YAH is unconditional! Although many will experience His punishments for disobedience. He said He protects those who love and seek Him, and He also said we show our love through obedience which is greater than sacrifices. Life is simply a test and everything in which we partake is being recorded. To fear YAH and keep His commandments has been the most necessary pledge of allegiance from the beginning and to love our neighbor as ourselves has been the bar set in which our hearts may be measured and judged. For Matthew 7 1&2 says with what Judgement you judge others you will be judged. Rev 20:13 verifies the dead are judged by their works. And Mark 7:9 prophesied of us leaving the commandments of YAH for traditions of man. Caution to anyone struggling with the importance of true Israel, the apple of YAH's eye. Luke 10:16 Messiah said he that heareth you heareth me; and he that despises you despised me; and him that despised me despises Him who sent me. The Bible is truth; religion is a lie. Choose you this day whom you will serve and make your calling and election sure. Love is truth, and YAH is love. YAH means what he says and he only says what he means for his word will not be void. The covenant is priority there is no other way, YAH is our mighty one for we must meet him at the door by these directions he gave. Everything that disagrees with His truth is of the deceiver. The fear of YAH is the very beginning of wisdom. Again, I say HalleluYAH!

ABOUT THE AUTHOR

In his first book *Disease to Freedom*, Cody Mitchell wrote about his life changing journey with health and medicine. Now using his time to write about his deeper understandings in regards to the bible, religion, and god. Born and raised in Arizona, Cody is a son, brother, uncle and friend to all of those seeking to find higher ground in this perilous time.

www.ingramcontent.com/pod-product-compliance
Lightning Source LLC
LaVergne TN
LVHW021624080426
835510LV00019B/2743